Little Dogs Rock! II

Miniature Schnauzer

Whiskers

by Margaret Fetty

Consultant: Susan Bias
Schnauzer Friends for Rescue and Adoption

BEARPORT
PUBLISHING

New York, New York

Credits

Cover and Title Page, © Gina Callaway/Shutterstock; TOC, © katielittle/Shutterstock; 4, Courtesy of Virginia Hyatt; 5, Courtesy of Virginia Hyatt; 6, © Month of September, Wertinger, Hans (ca. 1470-1533), Germanisches Nationalmuseum, Nuremberg, Germany Scala/Art Resource, NY; 7, © J.L Klein & M.L Huber/Biosphoto/Peter Arnold; 8, © Jerry Shulman/SuperStock; 9T, © Yan Wen/Shutterstock; 9B, © SuperStock RF/SuperStock; 10, © Robert Winslow; 11, © J.L Klein & M.L Huber/Biosphoto/Peter Arnold; 12L, © Courtesy of the Sparacino Family; 12R, © Eugene Choi/iStockphoto; 13, © Brinkmann Bernd/Biosphoto/Peter Arnold; 14T, © Sandra Wilson/Gtphoto; 14B, © Sandra Wilson/Gtphoto; 15L, © Laura McElroy; 15R, © Mary Altaffer/AP Photo; 16, © Cheryl A Ertelt; 17, © Nature PL/SuperStock; 18, © Isobel Flynn/Alamy; 19, © Robert Winslow; 20T, © J.L Klein & M.L Huber/Biosphoto/Peter Arnold; 20B, © Chris Brown/Alamy; 21T, © Robert Winslow; 21B, © Laura McElroy; 22L, © Connie Summers/Paulette Johnson; 22R, © Connie Summers/Paulette Johnson; 23L, © Arco Images GmbH/Alamy; 23R, © Robert Winslow; 24, © Pets by Paulette; 25, © Juniors Bildarchiv/Alamy; 26, Courtesy Everett Collection; 27, © Arco Images GmbH/Alamy; 28, © Chris Brown/Alamy; 29, © Jerry Shulman/SuperStock; 31, © suttisukmek/Shutterstock; 30, © Alfredo J. Correa/Shutterstock.

Publisher: Kenn Goin
Senior Editor: Lisa Wiseman
Creative Director: Spencer Brinker
Original Design: Dawn Beard Creative
Photo Researcher: Amy Dunleavy

Library of Congress Cataloging-in-Publication Data

Fetty, Margaret.
  Miniature schnauzer : whiskers / by Margaret Fetty.
    p. cm. — (Little dogs rock II)
  Includes bibliographical references and index.
  ISBN-13: 978-1-936088-20-1 (library binding)
  ISBN-10: 1-936088-20-7 (library binding)
  1. Miniature schnauzer—Juvenile literature. I. Title.
  SF429.M58F48 2011
  636.755—dc22
                    2010010636

For more information, write to Bearport Publishing Company, Inc., 101 Fifth Avenue, Suite 6R, New York, New York 10003. Printed in the United States of America in North Mankato, Minnesota.

062010
042110CGC

10 9 8 7 6 5 4 3 2 1

Contents

Play Ball!

Eight-year-old Chris loved playing baseball, but he didn't think he would ever be able to throw a ball again. A serious medical problem had forced doctors to remove one of his arms. Luckily, Chris was fitted with a **prosthesis** to replace the arm. However, the **physical therapy** to learn to use the new arm was so painful that Chris almost gave up. That's when his nurses came up with a plan to encourage him to keep working. They would introduce him to a special miniature schnauzer named Say-dee.

Say-dee is a **therapy dog**. She visits patients in hospitals and nursing homes. Her job is to make these people feel better and help them practice skills that will make their bodies stronger.

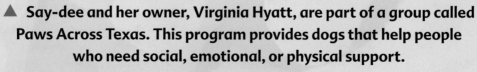

▲ **Say-dee and her owner, Virginia Hyatt, are part of a group called Paws Across Texas. This program provides dogs that help people who need social, emotional, or physical support.**

When Say-dee and her owner, Virginia Hyatt, first met Chris, Virginia said, "I hear you like to play baseball. Say-dee likes to play, too." Then she held out a ball to Chris.

Slowly and with great concentration, Chris grasped the ball with his prosthetic arm and tossed it. Like a silver streak, Say-dee ran and jumped up to catch the ball! Chris smiled and said, "She's good!" With Say-dee's help, Chris soon began to enjoy throwing the ball just as he had before he lost his arm.

◀ Say-dee is often dressed up when she goes to visit patients and students. She has more than 50 costumes, including those of a unicorn, a bee, and a rabbit. Say-dee and Virginia have spent more than 20,000 hours volunteering in hospitals, schools, and nursing homes.

A German Farm Dog

Just like her **ancestors**, Say-dee is a working dog. However, the kind of work she performs is much different than the kind of work her ancestors did. The first schnauzers were much bigger than Say-dee. At about 19 inches (48 cm) tall, they worked on farms in Germany in the 1500s. They had two important jobs. The first was to guard the **livestock**. The second was to kill mice and rats that carried deadly diseases.

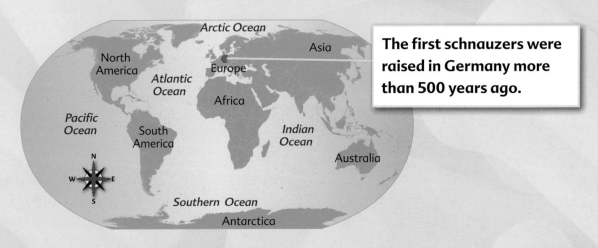

The first schnauzers were raised in Germany more than 500 years ago.

A German farm ▶ in the 1500s

Over time, farmers wanted smaller schnauzers that would be just the right size to follow rats and mice into small holes in the ground. So they **bred** the schnauzers with tiny affenpinschers (AH-fuhn-*pin*-sherz) and poodles. The new smaller dogs looked and worked the same as the bigger schnauzers—except they were now only 14 inches (36 cm) tall. Around 1899, farmers started calling this breed "miniature schnauzers."

The first schnauzers were considered perfect hunters because the hair on their noses, legs, and stomachs protected them from the sharp teeth and claws of the **rodents** they went after.

▲ **Affenpinschers are about 10 inches (25 cm) tall and were raised to hunt rats.**

Whiskers and More

Most miniature schnauzers raised today don't hunt rats and mice. However, their hair is still an important feature of the **breed**. These little dogs are best known for their whiskers. The long, thick hairs, which grow around their noses and on their chins, can be about four inches (10 cm) in length. They also have large, bushy eyebrows that frame their dark brown eyes.

▲ The breed name *schnauzer* comes from the German word *schnauze*, which means "muzzle" or "snout." The dogs got the name because of the whiskers around their noses.

These small dogs don't just have hairy faces. They have very hairy bodies, too. Long hair called a skirt grows on their stomachs. They also have patches of fuzzy, long hair covering their legs.

The long hair, especially the whiskers, makes the miniature schnauzer stand out from other dog breeds.

whiskers

fuzzy leg hair

skirt

The long hair found on a miniature schnauzer's eyebrows, stomach, and legs are called its furnishings.

Some owners may ▶ shorten or cut off the whiskers and furnishings of active miniature schnauzers.

The Double Coat

The whiskers and furnishings aren't the only unique characteristics of the miniature schnauzer. The little dog has a very special **coat**, which is made up of two layers of hair. The hair closer to the body, which is thick and soft, is the undercoat. It keeps the miniature schnauzer warm.

The undercoat keeps a miniature schnauzer warm in the winter.

The outer hair, or topcoat, is coarse and stiff. It helps keep the dog clean by protecting it from dirt and water. Surprisingly, with all this long hair, the miniature schnauzer doesn't **shed** very much.

Since miniature schnauzers don't shed very much, they often make good pets for people who have **allergies**.

▲ **The miniature schnauzer's coat keeps the dog comfortable all year long.**

Coat Colors

A miniature schnauzer's coat comes in many colors. However, the **American Kennel Club** (AKC) has set a **standard** and officially recognizes only three coat colors.

The most popular official coat color is salt and pepper. These dogs have light gray or white whiskers and furnishings. The topcoats, however, can be either dark gray or silver. The color depends on the mixture of black and white hairs in the topcoat. The more black hairs there are, the darker the coat will be. The more white hairs, the more silver or light gray the coat becomes.

▼ A salt-and-pepper miniature schnauzer

▲ Some miniature schnauzers are white. Since the AKC doesn't recognize this color, these dogs can't compete in AKC dog shows but they can compete in other AKC events.

The AKC also recognizes miniature schnauzers that are black or black and silver. These dogs have black topcoats and undercoats. However, the black and silver dogs have light gray whiskers and furnishings while the black dogs have black whiskers and furnishings.

A black and silver miniature schnauzer

The American Kennel Club holds different kinds of events where dogs can compete for prizes and ribbons. In some shows, judges give an award to the dog that best follows the breed standard. In other events, a dog can get an award for being well behaved and following its owner's directions.

Looking Good

To keep a miniature schnauzer looking its best, an owner needs to **groom** the dog every six to eight weeks. One way to do this is to strip, or pluck out, the dead hairs by hand. This doesn't hurt the dog, and it lets new hairs grow that are the same color and **texture** as the old ones. Then the whiskers and furnishings are cut with scissors.

◀ **The groomer gets the dog's coat ready for hand stripping.**

To hand strip a dog, a groomer uses a tool called a stripping knife. It looks like a metal comb with a wooden or plastic handle.

Most pet owners, however, shave their dogs' coats with electric clippers and then use scissors to trim the whiskers and furnishings. Over time, the coarse hairs of the topcoat don't grow back and only the soft undercoat remains.

▲ To compete in an AKC dog show, miniature schnauzers such as this one must have both their topcoats and undercoats. These dogs must also be hand stripped.

▲ A miniature schnauzer should be brushed daily to keep its whiskers and furnishings clean and free of tangles.

More Than Hair

While the whiskers and furnishings are the most well-known features of the miniature schnauzer, the shape of its head and body are also characteristic of the breed. The head of the miniature schnauzer is rectangular in shape. The ears sit on top and fold over to make a V shape. Some owners **crop** the dogs' ears to make them stand up.

▲ The miniature schnauzer on the left has folded-over ears, while the miniature schnauzer on the right has cropped ears. In some places such as Great Britain, it is against the law to crop a miniature schnauzer's ears.

Though these dogs are small, they have strong bodies and wide chests. From the shoulder, a miniature schnauzer stands between 12 and 14 inches (30 and 36 cm) tall. It can weigh between 11 and 20 pounds (5 and 9 kg).

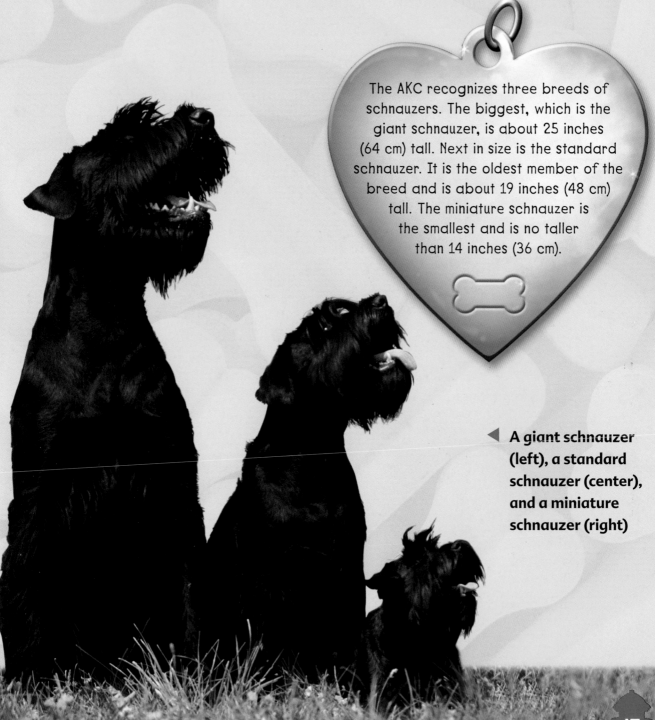

The AKC recognizes three breeds of schnauzers. The biggest, which is the giant schnauzer, is about 25 inches (64 cm) tall. Next in size is the standard schnauzer. It is the oldest member of the breed and is about 19 inches (48 cm) tall. The miniature schnauzer is the smallest and is no taller than 14 inches (36 cm).

◄ **A giant schnauzer (left), a standard schnauzer (center), and a miniature schnauzer (right)**

Getting Along

Miniature schnauzers may be small, but they have big personalities. These spirited dogs are very loving to their families, and they are happiest staying close to people they know.

It is best to introduce miniature schnauzers to as many people, places, and things as possible before the age of five months. After that, it's harder for them to get used to new experiences or changes.

▼ **Miniature schnauzers love spending time with their owners.**

Miniature schnauzers are very eager to please their owners, so they are quick to learn good manners. However, it's important for owners to carefully train their dogs so that they can get along with cats, others dogs, and people other than their owners. Potential owners should be aware that even a well-trained miniature schnauzer can be stubborn at times. They must continue to reward the dog with praise so it will be well behaved all the time.

To train a miniature schnauzer, an owner rewards the dog with praise and sometimes even a treat.

Traits of Old

While most miniature schnauzers no longer work on farms, many of today's dogs have some of the same **traits** that their ancestors had. For example, miniature schnauzers still love to hunt. They will chase and catch anything small that moves. If they aren't on a leash, they will run after birds or squirrels.

Miniature schnauzers can quickly cover a long distance without getting tired.

The first schnauzers were used to dig out rats and mice that hid in holes in the ground. Miniature schnauzers still show a strong urge to dig, even if there are no small animals around. Sometimes they even scratch the ground before lying down.

Today's miniature schnauzers also communicate in the same way as their relatives—by barking. These dogs often bark when they see unfamiliar people and animals or if they hear strange noises. They also use their voices to express their thoughts and feelings. They will grunt and groan if they are unhappy. They will say "woo-woo, roo-roo" when they are happy or excited.

Miniature schnauzers enjoy playing with toys because they remind the dogs of the little animals that they like to chase.

Miniature schnauzers ▶ are very vocal dogs.

A Healthy Breed

Though these happy, active dogs are generally healthy, they should visit a **veterinarian** once a year for a checkup. There are a few illnesses and other medical conditions that are common to the breed. For example, some miniature schnauzers get **cataracts** as they age. When this happens, a milky film covers their eyes, making it hard for them to see.

Miniature schnauzers may also have skin problems. They may get rashes, **blackheads**, or flaky skin.

▲ **This miniature schnauzer is getting eye medicine.**

A miniature schnauzer ▶ getting a checkup

Miniature schnauzers gain weight easily, too. To keep these dogs in the best health, owners must watch how much food their pets eat and never give them food from the dinner table. They should also exercise their dogs every day.

▼ **An owner and her miniature schnauzer dancing**

▲ **It's important for miniature schnauzers to exercise daily.**

For exercise, some miniature schnauzers and their owners dance. Known as "freestyle," the owner and dog follow set steps as they move to music. Many go to shows where they compete against other teams.

Little Puppies

All puppies are small, but miniature schnauzer puppies are extremely little. Most newborns weigh between four and seven ounces (113 and 198 g)—about the same size as a small container of yogurt. At first, the pups don't have long hair. It takes six to eight weeks before their whiskers and furnishings start to grow in. They also have darker coats than their parents. Their coats will grow lighter as they get older. For example, a puppy that has a very dark coat may become a salt-and-pepper color when it's an adult.

A mother miniature schnauzer (middle) with her seven-week-old puppies

Miniature schnauzer puppies need to stay with their mothers for about eight weeks. During this time, they build up their strength and learn to walk and play. Then most pups are adopted by families and become pets.

Miniature schnauzers are born with long tails. Their tails are often cut, or **docked**, when the dogs are about three to five days old.

The tail of this miniature schnauzer was not docked.

Perfect Pets

Besides being a loving, loyal dog, the miniature schnauzer makes a perfect pet for a family because of its tiny size. Since they are small, they can live in city apartments just as easily as in big houses. While these dogs are active and like to run outside, they are just as happy playing fetch or tug-of-war with their owners indoors.

Even **celebrities** are big fans of these dogs. For example, actors Bill Cosby and Bruce Lee have owned miniature schnauzers. Boxing champion Sugar Ray Leonard also has a salt-and-pepper miniature schnauzer named Kit.

Miniature schnauzers usually live for about 14 years.

Actor Bill Cosby has ▶ owned a miniature schnauzer.

It's not hard to understand why people choose these wonderful little dogs as pets. They may look small, but they are supersized in heart and spirit!

▲ **A miniature schnauzer enjoying a beautiful day with its owner.**

Miniature Schnauzers at a Glance

Weight:	11–20 pounds (5–9 kg)
Height at Shoulder:	12–14 inches (30–36 cm)
Coat Hair:	Two layers—a soft undercoat and a coarse, stiff topcoat
Colors:	Miniature schnauzers come in many colors, but the AKC recognizes only three: salt and pepper, black, and black and silver
Country of Origin:	Germany
Life Span:	15 years
Personality:	Happy, active, loving, loyal, smart, curious, good watchdog

Best in Show

What makes a great miniature schnauzer? Every owner knows that his or her dog is special. Judges in dog shows, however, look very carefully at a miniature schnauzer's appearance and behavior. Here are some of the things they look for:

rectangle-shaped head

ears set high

eyes are dark brown, oval-shaped, and set high

coat must be stripped; colors can be salt and pepper, black, or black and silver

tail is docked and carried up high

strong chest

hair on stomach

thick hair on legs

Behavior: should be alert, energetic, and friendly

Glossary

allergies (AL-ur-jeez) medical conditions that cause people to become sick after eating, touching, or breathing things that are harmless to most other people, such as dog fur

American Kennel Club (uh-MER-i-khun KEN-uhl KLUHB) a national organization that is involved in many activities having to do with dogs, including collecting information about dog breeds and setting rules for dog shows

ancestors (AN-sess-turz) relatives who lived a long time ago

blackheads (BLAK-hedz) black specks that form on the skin when a small amount of oil blocks the skin's pores

bred (BRED) mated dogs from specific breeds to produce young with certain characteristics

breed (BREED) a group of dogs that look very much alike

cataracts (KAT-uh-*rakts*) a cloudy film that can grow on the lenses of people's or animals' eyes; can cause blindness

celebrities (suh-LEB-ruh-*teez*) famous people

coat (KOHT) the fur on a dog or other animal

crop (KROP) to remove the outer or upper part of a dog's ear to make it stand up

docked (DOKT) cut off

groom (GROOM) to keep an animal neat and clean

livestock (LIVE-*stok*) animals raised on a farm or ranch, such as sheep and cows

physical therapy (FIZ-uh-kuhl THER-uh-pee) the use of exercise and equipment to heal an injury to the body

prosthesis (pross-THEE-siss) a device, sometimes made from metal and plastic, that replaces a missing body part

rodents (ROH-duhnts) a group of animals with large front teeth that includes rats, mice, squirrels, and chipmunks

shed (SHED) to lose hair or fur

standard (STAN-durd) the description of the "perfect" dog in each breed

texture (TEKS-chur) the way something feels when touched

therapy dog (THER-uh-pee DAWG) a dog that visits patients in hospitals and nursing homes to cheer them up and make them feel more comfortable

traits (TRATES) qualities or characteristics of a person or animal

veterinarian (*vet*-ur-uh-NER-ee-uhn) a doctor who cares for animals

Bibliography

Morris, Desmond. *Dogs: The Ultimate Dictionary of Over 1,000 Dog Breeds.* North Pomfret, VT: Trafalgar Square Publishing (2002).

Pisano, Beverly, and Gloria Lewis. *Miniature Schnauzers.* Neptune City, NJ: T.F.H. Publications, Inc. (1995).

Read More

Furstinger, Nancy. *Miniature Schnauzers (Dogs Set VI).* Edina, MN: Checkerboard Books (2005).

Moustaki, Nikki. *Miniature Schnauzers (Animal Planet Pet Care Library).* Neptune City, NJ: T.F.H. Publications, Inc. (2008).

Tagliaferro, Linda. *Therapy Dogs (Dog Heroes).* New York: Bearport Publishing (2005).

Learn More Online

To learn more about miniature schnauzers, visit
www.bearportpublishing.com/LittleDogsRockII

Index

About the Author

Margaret Fetty lives in Austin, Texas, with her two miniature schnauzers,
Cabo and Tristian. All three enjoy long runs in the park.